Finding True Love

Finding True Love

Natalie Maxberry

authorHOUSE®

AuthorHouse™
1663 Liberty Drive
Bloomington, IN 47403
www.authorhouse.com
Phone: 1-800-839-8640

Published by AuthorHouse   01/03/2013

ISBN: 978-1-4772-9601-1 (sc)
ISBN: 978-1-4772-9627-1 (e)

TABLE OF CONTENTS

In Memory Of My Parents

I ALWAYS WATCHED my mother wash. She would hang the clothes outside on the clothes line in the summer time and in the basement in the winter. When they were dry, I would watch her fold and then stack them in individuals piles . . . mine, my sisters, my dad's, hers. She would then put them in our drawers. (So much love). My father woke me up for school each and every day while my mother was in the kitchen preparing breakfast. Our parents sent us to Winchester Kentucky every single summer for some of the best days of our lives. I remember the good times the adults had together when our parents came to take us back home. I would sometimes go with my mother to my uncle's place. A bar/restaurant, my father's second job. Countless times I watched my dad work and eye every man in the room to not look my way while I ate hamburgers and fries. Both my parents worked two jobs to make ends meet and to be able to give us the things we needed and most of what we asked for. (So much love). We always had a variety of food to eat and always had a home cooked meal. We grew up in a nicely furnished six bedroom home in the same community I have purchased my home in. I remember their talks with me about what and what not to do in life and how to handle myself. How a woman behaves and what men expect. They were the best parents they knew to be as they raised their five daughters. They were a very strong example of how to keep a home together. How to keep a family together and how to keep a marriage together. (So much love).

They loved me and their entire family until the day they died. I was right by their side the moment they each took their last breath. That's how much I love them. They celebrated their forty eighth anniversary before passing away. My mother passed away first. My dad remained her husband until the day he died . . . he never remarried. In their memory I work hard attempting to at least (try) to live up to their legacy. I live each day to please God as they taught, and, in doing so, I hope my parents are pleased as well. A lot of us had parents like this, and, we all need to strive to be more like our parents. It all starts with love. Let us get started.

Introduction

THIS BOOK WAS written for single black men and women, but, all single men and women can benefit as well. Enjoy and may we all be pleased with the results. I would like to open by simply saying, we are family. By blood, by spirit, by faith. However it comes about, you are my people and I am yours. Unfortunately, a lot of family members have problems finding real true love. Year after year many of us suffer with loneliness of not having a soul mate or the unhappiness of being in a bad, unhealthy relationship. When there are problems, we look for solutions, but, in order to find solutions, we must go to the root of the problem. Correct. When it comes to love and the male, woman relationship and finding the root of the problem, going to the core of our failed and unsuccessful attempts at finding love, well, it gets a little messy. A little embarrassing. Because we are family though, we care about one another. When you know better you can certainly do better and if some of us have answers to some of the problem, there really is an obligation to share what we know. Correct.

Of Course, I am saying all that to say . . . here is my attempt to share what I have learned in my life span. I do pray that it is helpful. Once we work through some if our issues on an individual basis, things will be okay. Those of us struggling year after year, relationship after relationship, promise me you will keep reading until you reach the end of the book. Keep reading the important points that make you mad. The points that make you feel bad, that make you feel sad . . . those are probably the areas you are having the toughest time in, so, just keep reading. Believe me, we are all struggling somewhere, somehow. Don't worry about how rough or how tough I come at certain subjects in the pages to follow, or how raw I may be. My intention is to help us in our battle to find true love. I pray that God will guide this pen and in the end we will be one step closer to finding our mate. So let us open our hearts and mind. Let us dig in and see what we can find out, something we didn't know. One more thing to add to our pool of knowledge. One more thing to make us a little wiser as we prepare to open up our souls to receive real love. From my heart to yours. Now let us go to work.

Purpose

———

I AM SINGLE but I am hoping. Praying for a mate. Someone to settle down with, marry and share a nice and successful life with. I believe that someone special is searching for me too, but, before I meet them. Before they show up at the door, let me make a check list similar to like when I go shopping at the store. I need to know if I'm really prepared. Okay . . . My wardrobes together. I may have a good looking home and possibly a nice size bank account. These things are important but more importantly . . . is my thinking straight. Am I really clear. Am I truly ready for a good partner, truly ready for a good mate. Okay . . . let's not panic. Let's be cool. Let's stop for a minute and put on our serious face. Now, I'm tired of the games and waddling in worldliness, and, yes I really am ready to commit. I'm ready for faithfulness. I'm willing to make this great sacrifice to be and come clean. I will cook, wash, and sometime stay up through the night. Run around all day to keep things right. Relationships are work not just all fun. Realizing the work I put in is not just for the one of you but for the both of you. That what I'm asked to do, expected to do will in the end help pull us through. That everything, all of it pays off like a million dollars in your pocket when you see you and your mate coming along, you're a happy couple. When the two of you are bonding, planning, staying together. When you roll through whatever obstacles that come your way. When you're able to laugh, sing and dance wrapped in one another's arms. When you're blessed with a companion that you love and would die for . . . tell me this, who really can ask for anything more. Once we realize there is nothing more important in life than to do as God said which is to meet and then wed. Once we really understand this . . . there is nothing else to be said.

SECTION ONE

My Prayer

I AM WHO I am because it's who God blessed me to be. Through my trials and struggles I've learned more of me. What I should and shouldn't do. The right and wrongs in life. The do's and don'ts to avoid unnecessary strife. Now that that parts done, I can move on to be the greatest part of me. The part that God created through my past and the hard times He bestowed upon me. The part that will allow those experiences I've had to be put aside. The part that is now ready to become openly exposed to the good things God has in store for me. The part that will allow me to let go of the old and become the marvelous person that I am. The part that will become a man or a woman depending on the gender I'm born in. A strong man. A strong woman. God's man. God's woman. Let's pray that God continues to lead our way to ensure that we're all headed towards a beautiful, wonderful, extraordinary destiny.

In his Name

Amen

LOVE AND UNDERSTAND YOURSELF FIRST . . . THEN KNOW WHAT TO LOOK FOR

I KNOW WE all know or at least have heard of couples that met when they were five or seven years old. Certainly there have been couples who met in high school and all other young ages who stayed together. When you see or hear of them today, they are still together. Ever wonder how that happens. It's because we don't all meet our mates at the same time in life. Some are blessed to meet at an early age, some meet when they are thirty, fifty and even older. Whenever it happens. When it's true love . . . it's a true blessing from God. True from Webster's Dictionary is—faithful in allegiance, true from fraud or deception, constant, loyal, good, pious, staunch, steadfast. I would like to mention at this point that most of us at whatever age have experienced being in love, but, were they truly in love with us? If so, were we truly in love with them? A relationship is not a one man or one woman situation . . . it takes two. One just won't do. For those of us who haven't been blessed with true love, let's try to explore and see if maybe we can learn some new tools to help bring true love our way. Into our world.

Picture times you have gone into Walmart or any store that basically sells everything. You walk in with absolutely no idea of what you want. Most likely you will come out with whatever the store sells and probably things you don't even need. In other words, almost a complete waste of time and money. If you know what you want when you go in you are narrowing the madness down. (Women Want) chips, juice, fish, dress, purse, earrings, shoes, watch. (Men Want) chips, juice, fish, suit, tie, belt, shoes, watch. This is pretty specific. But, if women want . . . one bag of salsa sun chips, one gallon of orange juice, five lbs. of whiting fish, a beige ankle length dress, a beige pair of earrings, chocolate brown leather pumps, chocolate brown leather purse, a gold watch-face trimmed with rhinestones. Men want . . . one bag of salsa sun chips, one gallon of orange juice, five lbs. of whiting fish, a beige suit, beige bow tie, chocolate brown leather belt, chocolate brown leather dress shoes, a gold watch with a chocolate brown face. This is completely specific. Now both the man and the woman know exactly what to look for when they enter the store. The process of elimination. It works the same way when considering our soul mate. It works the same way in our decision for one person over the other if a choice needs to be made. The question is, are they who my souls searching for? Is it who I need in my life? Remember that want and need are two altogether different things. Sometimes we want things we don't need and that are not even good for us. A need is a necessity like clothes in the winter time. Maybe not the most beautiful outfit or brand name, but, warm, doing its thing, not playing games in their responsibilities. Caring for your health and well being. There to serve you in a meaningful way. The person may not be the best looking person in the world, but they are reliable and they handle their business concerning you. They don't make a mess out of their own lives and therefore won't make a mess of yours. Can you grow and prosper together? Chances are if they are doing well when you meet, the two of you will most likely do well together. It's the standard you both already set for yourselves before you even met. If you were already holding your fort down, I don't see why you wouldn't be able to do it together. Especially if you're praying. Especially if you're asking God for His help. For His guidance.

Know what you're looking for going in. Not too many emphasis on tall, short, skinny, fat, light, dark, cute, ugly. Rather honest, dependable, trustworthy, for both men and women. Providing and handling respectable good business. Women. It is the man's responsibility and obligation to provide so that's a given, but, if he is into the wrong type of business we will visit the Justice center and prison cells on a regular. Gains and properties confiscated at any given point. You're constantly looking over your shoulders because your man's not living right. Because your man's not practicing good business. You, him, the children and everyone else concerned deserves better. Know what you want going in. If you find someone with all the qualities you need; and they are the right height, color, size, and some of the other physical traits we want in a person . . . then that's just blessing on top of blessing, and isn't God good? We have to take the time to know ourselves in order to know what type person would be most pleasing to us. What type person is best for us. Have a clear idea of who you are before attempting to will someone into your world. This is the second step. The very first step is to love yourself before attempting to love someone else. First things first. Love yourself first. Taking the time to know, love and understand yourself first helps us know what we need in a mate. If we haven't taken the time to get to know and love ourselves, in most cases the wrong person for you shows up, and, because we don't have a clue on how to choose a mate, we fall for it. Hook, line and sinker. Eventually ending up regretting the day we met, but, in a lot of cases, we try very hard to fit them in and to make them apart of our life. A lot of us even go so far as to marry them. In these cases, they are very happy with you because they knew what they wanted and they got you. You on the other hand want to throw up, everyday. Be sure to pray for the right mate so that we won't pray the wrong mate into existence. These are some things you should be asking yourself while getting to know and understand yourself:

1. What do I need in a mate

2. What don't I need in a mate

3. What age bracket

4. What lifestyle

To know what type mate we need we have to know ourselves first. You have to know what you like. What you like in a person.

In a personality. What we like and dislike in life. What we want out of life. What we don't want. What we can tolerate. What we can't. This is to help find out if you will have anything in common with the person whenever you meet. Whenever you do meet someone it's totally mandatory to figure out if the two of you have anything in common. Now . . . I'm just going to go ahead and put this out there . . . these discoveries need to be made before sex. In fact there are some more discoveries to be made also and they are done before sex too. As a matter of fact . . . everything is before sex unless sex is all you're looking for. Otherwise when sex is not in the right order, disappointment and broken hearts are the results, and, most of us have had this experience entirely too many times. Both men and women. So let's hold off on all the physical and let's get back to the commonalities. Things in common are absolutely essential to a good relationship. It is important to know yourself and don't settle for someone who doesn't have anything you need in a mate. It is important that you love yourself, because, when you love yourself you won't go for some of the foolishness some people come with. Plus. The inner love you have for yourself will get your mates attention, penetrate their heart and draw them directly to you. It may also draw others, so be clear in your thinking, in your prayers. Be careful in your choice . . . don't settle for someone you have absolutely nothing in common with. A few more tips on this subject before we move on.

1. If you don't want someone who drinks, parties, and hangs out, don't look in the bars and disco clubs for your mate. That's where they are in their life.

2. If you care about your health and physical well being you may want to look for someone at the gym, the trail or fitness center.

3. Men. You may want to check to see if she ever even heard of a kitchen or if the only place she has ever eaten in her life has been in a restaurant. Hint. If the restaurant is all she knows, she probably can't cook, doesn't cook, won't

cook. Women. The reason I threw this in is because men love home cooked meals. Could be a tie breaker. (Smile). For real though.

4. If you are looking for a mate that loves, respects, and serves God, you may not want to date someone on the corner gang banging. A woman may not want a man pimping women, or, it wouldn't be too smart for a man to choose a woman who's known to sleep around. God, at least at this point is not their priority. Yes these worldly people can change and some of them will, but, change takes a long time. For a person to really become different it cannot happen overnight. If you have already dealt with yourself and you are really ready for your mate . . . if Gods willing, your mate is ready for you. They won't be caught in the middle of the above activities. They will have it together and are as clear as you on what they need. We must have the important critical things like those mentioned in common with our source of interest. We must always use common sense when choosing or accepting the source into our lives. Always keep in mind that opposites attract and that's why men love women, women love men. Keep in mind also that evil is the opposite of good. Good people . . . be very careful not to fall for the wicked, they are very persuasive. Once they are inside your heart, inside your home is when it dawns on you that you have made a mistake. You won't have anything in common-likes, dislikes, wants, needs. There will be no harmony. Be clear. Be careful with your choice. Remember. We are trying to find a mate, not opposition. Our mate, not an enemy. Common sense must be used and is always the key and you always want to attract someone in your league. Your lifestyle. Someone you can relate to. Someone you can talk to. Someone you can understand, respect, and will want to be with in time to come. Someone you will be proud to introduce to the world. Take some time to figure out what type mate you need based on who you are. Never forget and always remember to respect yourself, and, in return so will your mate be.

Me In The Mirror

REGARDLESS TO WHAT has been done. Regardless to what has been said. When I look in the mirror I see number one. I love my skin, my eyes, my eye lashes, my nose. I love my hands, my fingernails, my feet, my toes. I love my hair, my lips, my smile and my eyebrows. I love my legs, my elbows, my curves. I love my neck. I love my biceps. I love, love, love it, because, it's what God made. He made it all and it all belongs to me. I love my mind, my thoughts, my laugh, my personality. I love my thoughtfulness, my warmth, my caring, my sharing ways. I love that I'm bright, intelligent and eager to grow. Willing to accept positive change to help move me forward and see more awesome days. I love that even when the going gets tough, I continue to stand. I search and find my way through until times are better. I will continue to move forward until times are the best. I love that I'm strong and have confidence in myself. I love that I keep pushing and pushing without giving up. I will keep pushing until the day I make it to the top of my success and happiness. When I look in the mirror I see me. This is who I am. These are the wonderful ingredients all mixed together that make me. When I finally meet someone who is just like me. Someone who looks in the mirror and is proud of what they see. Someone who will love me for me because I'm the same reflection they see. Wow. What a union, and, we will both agree, that we love one another, because, you love you and I love me. We've both learned to accept and love who we are which makes us totally free from the mess and the way we were taught to be. At the same time we are working to become better and better to be the best people we can possibly be. We will keep growing, improving and reaching for the stars. We will both be so pleased and surprised when our lives wind up in a world of total beauty, tranquility and heavenly bliss. Amazingly. It all stems and comes from me loving me.

SECTION TWO

To All The Single Ladies

RATHER WE'VE THOUGHT about it or not. Rather we believe it or not. Rather we like it or not. Rather we respect it or not . . . men are the hunters, not women. I Know, I know . . . its "2012". I hunted my man down or pursued the relationship and got him. I don't have time to be sitting around with my fine self waiting for him to make a move and I know he'll want all this. Unless of course he's crazy or something. I'm too old and too desperate for all that foolishness, and, if I see someone I want I'm going to go after him. I'm giving it my best shot cause I know I look good. Look at this body. Who believes that old fashioned stuff about women not making the first move. Plus. What difference does it make anyway. And on and on and on. Women have become too aggressive and too out of order. Not for women because we're fine with our behavior, but in the man's eye. Sometimes you will run into an honest man and he'll tell you that, but in most cases, men won't. They just use your loose ways to their advantage. Guys maybe thirty five and younger think our behavior is fine because it's the only behavior they know. This is the world they were raised in, but, if we take things back which we will in a bit, we'll see where it all went wrong. How things went completely downhill. Women. Rather we realize it or not, this whole chasing men approach is actually back firing on us. It's reversing the whole man woman success story in so many, many cases. On so many levels. This is how we end up with men we now have in our homes. In our lives. Men that disrespect us. Respect from Webster's Dictionary-admiration, appreciation, esteem, favor, regard, concern. They lack respect for us and as a result, they cheat on us. Use us in whatever ways and if the truth be told, care about us maybe . . . only because we are having sex with them, but don't even really love us. When at the same time, we are totally and madly in love with them. Quietly and very sadly . . . throughout the entire time you're with him giving up blood, sweat and tears, he's praying and dreaming of a woman that he can respect. Even though he is involved with you, in his spare moments he is looking for a woman that he can appreciate and admire. If you chose and chased him, he doesn't have the respect a relationship needs to make a happy one. He doesn't appreciate you on the level you wish he did. He in most cases simply went along for the easy ride, but, not with you for the real or the right reasons. Let him choose you. From there you decide if he's right for you. Don't do things backward and waste your time, money and your effort in a backward relationship. A relationship going nowhere, or that's not headed in the direction you would like it to go. It isn't healthy. You're not happy. Approaching men is kind of like when and I'm sure we've all had this experience at some time in our life. When someone likes you a whole lot more than you do them. The more you resist them, the more you try to push them away, the more they like you. Okay. Let us reverse it. You have liked someone before more than they liked you and the more you liked them, the less they liked you. In both cases though if you ever noticed, the minute you stop stressing and trying so hard to win their affection is when they develop an interest in you. Reverse psychology. You don't want to ever get yourself in the position of trying to win a man's attention. Who needs that? When a man approaches you it's because he sees something in you of interest. Everything else stems from his interest in you. The right order of things. When you approach them . . . did they have an interest in you. Any kind of attraction to you, for you. Wrong order of things. Wouldn't you rather know that he's interested in you before you become involved with him. Or, chase him and years later you're still not married. For those who begged him into marriage, how happy are you. Let the men interested in you make the first move to get you. Let them come to you.

Anyone who doesn't approach you just simply means they are not the one for you. This is absolutely and perfectly fine, because the right man, your man will be one hundred percent for you. Let wrong men go. Let them go where they're going because, we're only looking for one man. The right man. Right. Again. We have to always keep common sense out front otherwise we will bring the wrong person into our heart. If a man doesn't approach you it's because he doesn't have an interest in you and therefore he is not your man. Your man will have total interest in you. Process of elimination.

Now you can run after men all you want and believe me . . . that's what your life will consist of. Running after men. Women. You know what I'm talking about and you know what I'm saying is true. Let the man choose you first and that puts you in control of the rest. Until our man does arrive, the only job we have is to become beautiful inside and out. At the same time we're also praying in our minds for the best man out there for me to step up. Well you know. The best is for the best. I mean because you do want your partner to be as equally whatever, whatever. Right. Of course all women want the best, and, we should . . . but guess what. So does he, just as he should. Besides being beautiful from my heart out, what else do I need to help me become a better me. A better woman. The best I can be.

I told you earlier that we would go back in time a little bit . . . so, here we go. Let's start with women forty, fifty and older. Most of our parents were married and stayed married. If they lived, they celebrated fiftieth and sixtieth anniversaries. Once when I was a customer service representative, I spoke with a woman on the phone and she said she and her husband had been married for seventy years. I know those days basically no longer exist, but, why. Before we go any further I will say that I personally know of several couples outside of my family and a couple within my family who have been married, not living together, but, married for thirty, thirty five years. I also know a couple who are friends to our family and they have been married for fifty five years. Hats off totally to all of them. They are all good examples for what we're trying to achieve with this book. All examples of the way all relationships should end up when two people take the time to know one another first. Have the important matters and issues in common secondly. When love steps in. When your loves been tested with certain situations and over a certain period of time. When you know deep in your heart that life wouldn't be right anymore if they were not in it. If they just never showed up again. When those thoughts and feelings are running through your heart and mind and in the blood pumping through your veins, the next logical step is to be wed. Make a commitment to the one you love. A generation or two ago, this was the normal way of life. Men and women being wed. What has happened. What has gone drastically wrong. It is all in how we handle ourselves as women these days in opposed to how women handled themselves in their day. I will explain. Women had a lot of pride and self respect back then. A lot more than most women today. Women carried themselves in a different way then. They had a lot of class. They dressed differently. With a lot of class. They thought different of themselves back then. Women had more dignity and their men responded accordingly. Of course there were lose women then and there always has been lose women, but, if you think about it . . . the lose women didn't get chose then and that's precisely why lose women don't get chose in this day and time. We don't get chose for wives because we're lose. One day stands and bootie calls yes, but no man wants a woman that any other man or all other men can have-whoever you choose to give yourself to in other words. Many women are lose, outrageous and without husbands. A man's woman is sacred to him and off limits to other men. You should require the same of him. Otherwise don't even try for a relationship . . . you're still the one night stand-bootie call girl. Be sure to let him know that up front and, that type man you may have. They are out there by the barrels just waiting on you to show up and offer yourself. The good thing for those who are a part of this type world but really want better for themselves. That really want more. That really prefer to be in a committed relationship that will ultimately lead to the altar, there are things we can do to help the process along. Here and now choices need to be made. Do we want to continue to be treated like the dirt beneath the soles of his shoes. Or demand his love and respect through correcting our own conduct. If we're looking to become someone's wife someday, we must first get it together and become wife material, just as you want him to do. It all starts with self respect. Men won't respect us if we're not respecting ourselves. Good men are not looking to marry women who hang out and walk the streets all hours of the night half dressed. Put on some clothes. This is also for your own safety and well being out here in this crazy, wicked world. Half dressed and the wrong type dress in general helps men to look at us in wrong ways. It helps add to wrong choices and as a result, more and more failed relationships. Lose dress and lose behavior are ways of the world and we need to be coming away from all this non lady like behavior. After all, all men should not have the privilege of enjoying all your beauty. Only one man has this right . . . your husband. Again. Keeping common sense out front. You don't want a man to choose you because you have beautiful sex and a beautiful body that he can't resist, but, he can't stand you. Your mind. Your thinking. Your wants and desires in life. Cover yourself up so he can think straight. Let him get to know you, not your body. If he loves you on the inside . . . well then, you're cooking with gas. (smile).

Next Subject:

Let me say this though before I go on. I know I'm coming strong and I'm not finished. It is really only because I care about the way our world is headed. The way our families are headed. Our entire society is falling apart and we all have a responsibility both men and women to try and salvage what we individually can. Okay. Back to work. When you are at home, worried, anxious and ready to have a nervous break down waiting for your man to finally get his behind home. He shows up at last at 3:00 and 4:00 in the morning. How do you feel. Do you have any respect for that mess or the mess he was doing til 4:00 in the morning, you don't. Rather he was out getting high with the boys. Gambling his money away. Sleeping with another woman. Hanging in the bar drinking his self to death. Or, sharing his time at a peep show with other women. Women that are doing for him what you should be doing, and he is giving his money to them. Whatever his reason is for rolling in your door at 3:00 or 4:00 in the morning is un excusable. Its disrespectful and unacceptable behavior in your eyes. This will be a mans exact, same reaction when you as his woman shows up at 4:00 am. Rather you were out getting high with your girls. Gambling your money away. Sleeping with another man. Hanging in the bars drinking yourself to death or at one of those parties where men dance around with their privacy all in your face. Whatever your reason is for rolling in your door at 3:00 or 4:00 in the morning is un excusable, disrespectful and unacceptable behavior. Ladies who don't have a man at this particular time but want one. If this is your behavior every weekend. Every other night, etc. Men observing you, men watching your conduct-good men that is consider this above behavior un excusable, disrespectful and unacceptable and look the other way for the other type woman. The other type man will choose you, but, not for wives. Get what I'm saying. If this is your world and you are satisfied, then you're satisfied. If you're not satisfied in the world you're in and you want more. You want a good man to settle down with and marry, you will need to start making some changes. Changes that will only make you a better woman. We should all men and women strive to be the best person we can be. Changes are necessary because we must change as we grow. It is like the equivalent of climbing Jacobs ladder. We start wherever we are but the goal is to reach the top. We don't want to stay down here playing around in mud with muddy men. Reach high. I know some of you say . . . I only do this stuff because he does and I'm just showing him how it feels. Well. You know when we were younger, when you would do something just because someone else did it. The feedback from our parents would be . . . if they jumped off a bridge, would you jump too. Same thing. We don't follow the leader to bad behavior. Behaviors that eventually grow into bad habits. We don't tit for tat, that's what children do. Grown, mature, intelligent women make grown, mature, intelligent choices and decisions for their life. When you really think about it you can't win because there is no win in it. Nothing to feel good about. Nothing to be proud of. In about ten or twenty years from now when you're broke down, played out. A house full of children without a dad around for financial or mental support. When all your men have left because they found women who have a lot more going for them. Then you will be proof, a living example of why things must change. Now. We're not going to wait for all that, we will be the stars we really are. We will start today, right now in fact moving our thinking around. Set your goals and make the changes that need to be made. We all have issues. We all have problems, me, and every one of us. Figure out what they are if you don't already know. Figure out how to solve them. Figure out how to get rid of them so that we can make more discoveries. So that when our man stands before us . . . we will be new and improved. The woman he is looking for. The best to be found, therefore he need not look one step further. See what I mean.

Next Subject:

Now we all know from our own experiences that hound dogs and no good men do everything rude under the sun. Unfortunately they used us to do their dirt. Now that that madness is all said and done. Now that we have made our mistakes and have learned from them. Now that we're moving forward striving to be good women, our focus is on good men. We know that men are the hunters . . . that they choose us. We then reply yea or nay. Did you know that good men watch us as well as the other, just in a different more respectful way. In a subtle type way. It is without all the whistling, hollering, patting, slapping, but, they watch. Did you know that that's what their born to do. That that's their nature. One of their responsibilities as a good man is to look out for Gods woman. Rather romantically or not. So don't ever think you're not being watched. When they are interested in us romantically, they study us. Sometimes you catch them looking, but, mostly they won't let you know unless of course you get chose. They are checking us out. They want to know who you are, the person on the inside. They want to know how we live. They want to know what we're about. They are searching for commonalities because really they want someone too to settle down with. Just like you do. When we improve our conduct, our ways, its noticeable and even no good men are forced to step up their game. Believe me, they'll do it because now they have something to work for. So, be real careful. Be real clear cause both good and no good men will come at you then. The better we have it together, the better the variety to choose from will be. The better together we have it, the stronger the men have to come. Not necessarily in the type car he drives or his wardrobe and how well he dresses, but in integrity, loyalty and for their zest for the good things in life. His ability to want, desire and care for a wife. Kind of feel where I'm going. We help elevate men and it all depends on how elevated we are as a woman. Yes, once he becomes a man he looks for a woman. One of us. His woman takes him from moms hands. It then becomes him and his woman. One of us. So, stop playing yourself cheaply. Realize who you are and how important your contribution is to the circle of life. Rather our contribution has been good or bad. Whatever bad we've put out, we would like to correct from this day moving forward. Whatever good we have given to the world works in our favor. Now we know how important we are and the role we play in the man's sincerity to us. In relation to our own success and happiness. The more serious we are about ourselves, the more serious men will be about us. We set the stage on how things get played out by the way or the level of respect we have for ourselves. When you don't have any respect for yourself, men won't have any for you. When you have ultimate respect for yourself, men treat you like a queen. It's all in our hand. Now that we have this piece of the puzzle, let's move on. Decent women which is what we are should really be trying to make it to the house before night fall or before the late hours. This is really around the time you would like him to be in too, so, don't ask for more than you're willing to give. The environment becomes more dangerous at night. Crepes, freaks and wild animals hang out at all hours of the night, not decent human beings. You know of course that there is always an exception. If you really have somewhere to be, you have somewhere to be. Assuming though that somewhere is decent, you're decently dressed and you're conducting yourself decently. You never know, you could meet your mate on the way to where you're going or when you get there. Now we understand. If we're looking to attract a good man, we must first become a good woman, because as we know . . . first things first. Ladies. Before we continue to complain that there are no good men out there, we first have to become a good woman before we have the right to complain. Until then, know and realize that men will continue to complain that there are no good women out there. There is no difference between the two of us. We are both searching for the best. Everyone, both men and women have their work cut out, and, it is time for both men and women to go to work.

For women who have already landed a decent man, but, you are a woman whose not, well, you stand the chance of losing him if you don't work on getting yourself together. Good men are fed up just as good women are. One day a decent woman may catch his eye and he'll be gone. Commonalities are what make a relationship work. An individual's nature is at the top of the list. A good natured person coupled with an evil natured person is a miss match. So, we all need to work on getting things together before someone who has it together comes through and takes what we thought was ours. Sometimes, even though your man may be with you, he might not be happy. It gets tricky so let's be careful, tighten up our conduct and become the best woman we can be not the worst behaved on the entire street you live on. Men want to be proud of their woman just as you want to be proud of your man. When you are both proud of one another . . . wow what a relationship you have. One last thing and then we move on.

We meet him and he seems satisfactorily all over the place even down to treating you with utmost respect. Do we then turn around and disrespect him for respecting us. For example . . . he goes to open our door and we disrespectfully smart off with, I know how to open my own door. We know anyone with functioning hands and a brain can open the door. What is that other than rudeness and total disrespect to him. Allow him to respect you. If he shows you a nice evening, do we appreciate it or do we complain to him like a big whinny baby that you didn't go where you wanted to go and he didn't spend enough on you. He's cheap. Or do we appreciate his thoughtfulness, period. He didn't have to show any courtesy. No chivalry or spend any of his money on you, but, because he did . . . our response is, thank you. These are forms of kindness. When someone is kind to you the response is, thank you. If at the end of the night, he passes on coming in, do we disrespect him and ourselves by forcing too much too soon. Or, do we follow his lead so that we get the opportunity to see where he is headed in the days to come. Remember. Haste makes waste and patience is a virtue. Slow your row. Slow our thinking. Sometimes when a man won't go all the way with you or to whatever physical level you may want and desire, it could be that he is really feeling you and therefore he is trying to get to know you. He's trying to see if you two fit together. If you're the one for him. If this is the case, he won't try to use and take advantage of you. He won't come at you in a physical way. He's checking you out. He wants to get to know you better. We want the future we're dreaming and desirous of, not to be just a one night stand. Or to simply be his bootie call at 2:00 or 3:00 o'clock in the mornings for months or maybe even years to come. Be cool. Respect yourself. Allow him to respect you. Play it all the way out and see where he's going. Remember. Haste makes waste. Don't blow a possibility by moving too fast, too soon. Our bodies. Our sex are the most and the most important thing we can give a man. The most important outside of our brilliant minds. The mind comes first to see if our mind is compatible with his mind. Sex is the very last thing that should enter into the relationship equation. Once you absolutely feel in your soul that he is the one that satisfies your soul, the very next step is to know that he feels the same exact way about you. Real proof will be that he marry you and at that point we all agree that sex becoming a part of the equation is safe, appropriate, right. Anytime sex comes in before marriage, it is at your own risk because either of you really know where the relationship will end up. If it doesn't end at the altar with both of you committing to one another, he just becomes another man in your life you slept with. Keep in mind, every time we sleep with someone who isn't our husband . . . this man is taking what should be for our husband, and, our husband only. Why sleep with men that are here today and gone tomorrow. Why allow yourself to be used in this way. Why accept this penis and that one and then this one and then that one and on and on and on into your body. Into our system to rotate back and forth throughout your blood stream. Each one dumping their sperm, waste and children in you and they are not even your husband. Not only that, but, in time are no where even to be found while you continue to carry them around-like dead weight for life . . . along with the shame and disgust that come along with it. Do you really think that little of yourself, or, did you not even really think about the seriousness of the vulgarity you allow men to perform on you. Since we are the only channel a man can go through for sex, this makes us very valuable and priceless to men. That is if we don't lose all of our value by giving all of our valuables away. Those of us blessed to have diamonds, pearls, furs, minks, money . . . do we give them all away until there is nothing left. The answer is no. We are more valuable than anything else in God's creation, so says God, so, why then is it okay to give ourselves to any Tom, Dick or Harry. It is not okay. For all the good we do in our lives, we get blessed in good ways. For all the wrong we do in our lives, we get punished in ways that we can't even imagine, and, it is based on what we've done and how long we've been doing it. Gods command is marriage and then sex, not sleep around all the days of my life and never marry. Life gets real tricky so be real careful how you live. Just as we wouldn't give our gold and silver away just because, just because he looked at you. Because he said hi. Because he looks good. Because his car is pretty. Because you saw some money in his wallet. Or, even if you're horny. This is a man you need to learn. You need to know if he is right for you. If he is a good fit for you. Not, let's get busy, let's get physical. Nothing mentioned equates to giving him your body at first acquaintance or in the beginning stages of a relationship. Even if we think so, God doesn't and He knows men better than us. He created them . . . remember If we're not right for one another, we should find this out before sex, not afterward. While he still has respect for you. Take charge. Be careful. Be strong in your morals. Be sure not to put the cart before the horse by doing things backward when it comes to men. We have to protect ourselves. Treasure yourself just as you treasure your children. Your grandchildren. Treasure your sex just as you do your nice clothes. Your jewelry. Your furniture. Your money. Of course, sure, they can always get sex from the next woman or any woman who gives it out. The problem those women have though above many is, the sex doesn't mean much because truthfully and rather he even realizes it, he's looking for more than just sex. If he's any good that is. Good men are just like you, they are looking for love and companionship. He's searching for a special friend he can confide in. A woman he can trust. He knows if you gave or tried to give yourself to him in the first fifteen minutes, you'll give yourself to the next man you feel like having sex with. Good men don't share their woman with other men nor do they share themselves with other women. Good men are looking for good women. Not women who want whatever, whoever, whenever . . . simply because you lack discipline and strong self love. Good women are looking for good men. Not men who want everyone they see, again, due to no discipline. We have most certainly been raised by the devil himself to be made to think that this type conduct is fine. That it's okay. If we haven't already, we have to clean up our behavior if we want a clean man. Women must become good and well behaved morally if we expect to get and then keep a good man. Of course. Vise verse. Men must do the same. Its mandatory for both of us to get ourselves together.

When a man is courting or dating you, during the courting process, take this time to figure out what kind of man he really is. Is he someone I would like to spend my life with, not, how soon will we sleep together. Sleeping with a man should be the last thing on the agenda. If you don't take the time to find out who he really is, you could be sleeping with an uncle you haven't met yet. A rapist. Or. If you want marriage . . . a man who doesn't want marriage at all. Time spent together along with the right questions are the only way to find out the important things about him. Take your time and get to know who the man is and find out if he's even worth your time. Is he worthy of you. Do that before he breaks your heart. Before you give him the key to the house and the car. Before he gives you a baby. Before he gives you aids. Protect yourself. Remember to use common sense. If sex keeps popping up in the conversation, sex is really all he wants. Not marriage. To continue on with him is blocking the way for the right person. God gave us a brain and we certainly have to use it when it comes to men. We're looking for marriage not just someone to have sex with outside of marriage. Sex comes much later, not in the beginning of two people trying to get to know one another. Never mention marriage though, let him do that. If you bring it up he then knows marriage is what you want. If he doesn't want marriage and if he's no good, he could play you for the next ten years. Or, however long you allow it promising marriage every step of the way. When it's all said and done, he never marries you. He never intended on marrying you but because you let him know this is what you want . . . he used it against you. In order for him to hold on to you, he keeps lying to you with the fake promise of marriage. Secondly, you don't want to appear desperate. Desperate women aren't very appealing to men. Of course the consideration of marriage takes time to arrive at. Feelings evolve and develop, unless its love at first sight for both of you. If not, either one of you want to marry one another instantly. The relationship needs to grow. Things of importance takes time. Marriage is a very extremely important step in anyone's life. In fact marriage is the most important step two people can make. Take the time to learn important things about him. Take time to see if the important things they say are really true. Investigate some. See if he really is who he says he is in the first place. Check him out to the best of your ability. Find someone who knows him to see what type man he is. See if he really works at the particular job he says he works at. Take the time to find out if he's truthful or just a cold blooded liar looking for a woman to take care of him. Look out for yourself. Protect your heart. Use common sense when it comes to men. Once he has learned what he needs to know of you and he's interested in you on that level, he will bring marriage up. Even so and before you go bananas test his sincerity on marriage. Why does he feel he wants to marry you. Bring up a few of your faults just to see if he says so, that's neither here nor there. It doesn't change his feelings for you. Try a couple of things to push him off and see if he still stays. Test him to find out his level of sincerity for you. This is how a strong relationship is built. If nothing you do runs him off, maybe he's for you. If it doesn't pan out and you weren't too pushy, too anxious but showed signs of interest at the same time. If nothing becomes of the relationship, it's okay. Let him go. Tell him bye. Obviously he's not the one for you. If during this process he's already having sex with you. Living with you. Driving your car. Eating your food. He has access to your bank account whenever, however he pleases. Chances are, he won't marry you. Live with you for years to come . . . yes. Marry you . . . probably not. He probably doesn't respect you in the ways that he should either. You have heard the expression . . . why buy the cow if you're already getting the milk free. That was in the olden days. Now days, he is not only getting the milk, but, he owns the entire cow. In other words, you have given yourself and everything you own to someone who has not even committed to you and you're asking for respect. You have given him everything you have for absolute nothing in return, but, the hard work of trying to hold the relationship together. Good luck with that because, he won't respect you. This is the same equivalent as walking down to the bank in the morning, giving the banker all your savings, closing your account and walking out telling him to enjoy your money any way he sees fit. He will say . . . thank you very much! Thank you to your face and when you leave, say to himself, she must be a fool. Of course, in the end when your thinking becomes clearer, you are hurt and disappointed at yourself. Don't put the cart before the horse. You're always more important than anyone else, except, when you're raising little ones, when you're raising children, they always come first. When it comes to men, they won't have to buy the cow when they already own it. Translation. He doesn't have to marry us because he already has us. When he already has everything he needs and everything you have, you have nothing else to give him-you have already played your whole hand. Given all you have to give. Because he is not even your husband, he shouldn't even have any of it, and, he knows that. You have spoiled him. Now he uses you for the things you give him. He's already in heaven and in most cases, will not budge. In other words, he has no need for the altar. He already has everything he wants except one important thing . . . a woman he can respect. Sisters have a leach, a bum and a user. He's in heaven because he hit a lick, you on the other hand are in hell and are being used. It is because we go about the dating process backwardly. Don't let men play you. Don't dare let them use you. When a man is interested in you, he will begin to talk. Listen. Don't do a lot of interrupting him with your thoughts. Listen to what he has to say. The most important way to find out what type person he is, is, to listen to him. If you do discover that he is really not interested in marriage at all and you are. Next. For real because you are interested in marriage. He is going to waste your time and energy trying to change his thinking. Trying to change his thoughts about marriage. You should only involve yourself in courtships with possibility. The man you become involved with should at least want marriage. Right. If you want marriage but he doesn't, he can't be the man you're looking for. Common sense and, we move on. Just chalk the whole experience up as another learning tool. Each dating or courting experience, or each man teaches us something we need to know for our man when the time comes. Because you don't give him the car. The house. The children. Sex . . . hey. See you later. Next. No harm done. Right. The one we are looking for is out there somewhere. God made a mate for all of us. The only question is . . . when will we meet. Keep moving forward with your life and keep believing. When you meet someone who is interested in you and the feelings are mutual, ride the process out to be sure you're compatible enough. During this period of time, you are getting to know him. Ask the important questions. He is getting to know you as well. Be open. Be honest with him. If he still continues to come, continues to call. The two of you continue to harmonize. You seem to have a lot in common with the important things . . . he may be your match. Remember. Don't panic and lose control. Don't let your emotions take over and ruin a good thing. Continue to use your head. Remember. Hastiness will blow it . . . pace . . . pace . . . pace. Take your time and study your opponent. Just concentrate on making the right moves to ensure you win your man. Major Things You Need To Have In Common

1. Faith. Does he believe in and serve God. If not your lives may drift apart by all the worldly influences that can creep into the relationship if God is not at the base keeping you both on a straight and committed path to one another. Either of you want to be involved in the foolishness going on outside the home. Gods people are groomed in honesty, kindness, morals and will treat you well.

2. Does he like who you are. What you stand for. How you think. If not there is nowhere else for him to go but out the door. You and who you are is who he should love. You. Everything else is secondary. It won't work if he doesn't like you. Your essence.

3. Income. Does he have a regular, steady income. How much he earns is not everything. If his income is not what you wish it were, don't be quick to completely turn your back on a nice man who you have major things in common with.

Just because his income isn't quite what you expect, if the two of you are living and doing right, special blessings and opportunities will open up for you along the way. The person himself can't be replaced. Each person is their own unique self and there is not another. Even if you replace him with someone else, the new man may have more money but he won't be the same person. He won't have the same qualities. The same character. Incomes fluctuate up and down. In and out. The right person doesn't. One time opportunity. Don't give him away. If you're at this point in the relationship, you're at a good point. Sit down together. Put your heads together to see how things may be worked out. A second job for a period of time may be an option. Tuning in on hidden talents that could generate an income. Anything you do well enough that's good and right that could produce an income if cultivated. We should be headed towards entrepreneurship anyway so that our whole world and well being is not solely in someone else's hands. It's harder for a marriage to survive when one or the others total income is lost. In today's economy, loss of income at any point could very well become a reality. How many have already lost money in the stock market. We have to begin to prepare for the unexpected. Start working on something outside the box. In other words . . . step out of our comfort zone. Outside of our everyday dependency on our jobs, on this economy. Because of the economy, it is now becoming extremely mandatory that we find other avenues to make an income. Legal though people, legal. Everything has a consequence, so whatever we do . . . make it right. Make it good. This way, blessings will continue to flow. Therefore, whatever amount of an income you're working with, you will see progress. No matter how soon or how much later, things automatically improve. Patience. The forces who are God and His help step in when you're trying to live right. Even when you don't see big changes over night or even in quite some time, be patient. It's a virtue. Keep working and always remember that Rome was not built in a day. Most things really worth while usually don't happen instantly. Just continue to have faith. Continue to exercise your brilliance. Whatever amount of money you have, use it wisely. Make sure before you accept any man into your life and (men this goes for you as well) . . . make sure they spend their money wisely. You can't get ahead if one or the other is careless or wasteful when it comes to the budget. No matter how much you make, if one continues to blow money, you don't grow. Or you grow at a much slower pace. You end up being the one trying and working the hardest to maintain the budget. You end up being unhappy with feelings of defeat. When a spouse isn't on the same page when it comes to goals that benefit and move the family forward . . . needless to say, of course, this can lead to a failed relationship. Of course, failure is not the goal. While having this important discussion during your courtship, figure out who will be in charge of the budget. It could also be that you're both good at finances, and, in that case . . . both of you go to work building your empire. If though one simply doesn't get it, let them give a certain portion of their income for the advancement of the whole. Let the other handle the goals. This works the same with anything within the family. It's okay. It's alright because the point is, the family will grow. If you're not good with finances you're good at whatever you're good at, so, that's what you offer the household. Whoever does whatever best is what you should do.

4. What Do They Bring To The Table. Look to see what they have already accomplished in their life. This will help you figure out who he is. If a person just graduated from high school or college, unless they happen to be wealthy or rich, they won't have much. You will grow and achieve together. Someone in their thirties should at least have their own apartment. Their own car with thoughts of one day purchasing a home, their very own apartment building or something. In other words they should be on their way somewhere headed in the right direction in life. Even if you're back at home with your parents because whatever,

whatever didn't work out, they should have money saved. Their own business. Something headed in the right direction. Back in school or something going for himself. In other words a person at this age should have mapped out something for his life. If not, they may be just getting home from prison or they are someone wondering around and doesn't want anything in life. Of course, this would explain why they don't have anything. There could also be one other reason. They may be plain lazy and not willing to work for anything. To help someone coming home from prison to get on their feet is an individual choice. To settle for someone who doesn't want anything in life and the only thing they do have is what you worked for and gave them . . . well, not very smart. This type person turns around and is then envious of you because you provide for them the things they should provide for themselves plus some because they are the man. In the end, they don't really appreciate it because they don't really want anything. A no win situation. Needless to say, they should be out the door as soon as you can get it open. If a man is too lazy to care for himself, he is too lazy to care for you. Not to even mention children if you were to have some, or, if you already do. If a man doesn't want anything out of life, well. First of all that's very sad. There is so much goodness in life to have and for someone not to want anything speaks volumes. Here is the thing though . . . people who don't want anything simply don't want anything, and, those type people are out here. Once this character trait has been identified, stay far away from both type men. Life has much more to offer. They both need to reevaluate themselves and grow up. Men in their thirties should have something. Money saved. Something. These are signs and proof of where his monies going. How well he handles money. Of course, the older we get, the more accomplished we should be. In today's economy even if we're not able to buy and have like we did in the past, we want to be able to hold on to what we already have. If at all possible. This is not for the purpose of "Gold Digging" but a tool to measure his sincerity about his own life. If he is not serious about himself he may not take your plans, dreams and goals very seriously. Sit down. Talk. Find out if he has a business head. See if he is someone who wants something in life or if he is someone who gets paid every week and doesn't care about how or where his money is spent. He doesn't know how to make his money work for him. People who don't know the value of money blow money that should be used to accomplish worth while things. We need money, food and water set aside for rainy and harder days to come. We have homes and companies to purchase. Restaurants and schools to open. Stores and gas stations to buy. Anyone just blowing money isn't thinking very wisely. If they want to wise up but never really knew how or never maybe had the right encouragement is one thing. On the other hand. If this is how they are and they love being irresponsible . . . just blowing paycheck after paycheck . . . realize you will be spending your life with this same type irresponsible person. He doesn't understand or have any respect for money, and, you certainly won't understand or have any respect for the fact that he doesn't when one disappointment after the other takes place and when it's all said and done. This needless to say won't make a very happy home.

5. Dependability. Does he call and come when he says he will. Is he honest and dependable. You don't want to go through life with someone who doesn't respect you. Someone you can't trust. Someone who doesn't come through when they say they will or someone who never supports you. These behaviors if they continue to show up during the courtship . . . you may continue being stood up, you may continue to be all alone even after you're married. Pay close attention to his actions. Don't make excuses and over look bad behavior. We deserve to be treated as queens. Respect. Patience. Kindness. These are requirements from both men and women. We should be able to trust the words coming from one another's mouth. You should be able to trust and depend on one another in general. You should become one

another's best friend. Be reliable. Come through when you say you will.

If you're in a courtship, slow everything down until you've really had time to study him. Time to find out if he qualifies for you. Time to find out if you're really fit for one another. Be sure to play your hand with total respect for yourself and the relationship you're trying to build. What the two of you actually want, expectations of one another should actually be shared and discussed with one another.

If the above is going well and intact. If he makes you smile inside and out. If you feel safe and protected when he is around. You feel warm and cozy when he is near and he is on your mind when he is not. If he is caring and sharing towards you. If you feel good and secure in your position as his woman based on the love and respect he shows you under all circumstances. If you know deep down in your soul that you are the apple of his eye . . . because you have already tested him in different ways to make sure . . . maybe you have found your true love. The rest is personal and between the two of you. Keep God in mind and continue to pray every step of the way. Ask God to help you decide correctly. With His help and stamp of approval, the two of you will meet at the altar. Go girl. Mission accomplished.

When A Good Man Arrives

He walks across the floor looking good. Very debonair. You notice but try hard to ignore. Be cool and

see if its you he's interested in. Men like the chase so don't be too fast, not too anxious. Just continue

doing what you were doing before he came in. If its you he wants he will let you know. However,

whenever, he'll tell you so. Follow his lead and see where it leads. A good man, not the other, but, a

good man is looking for his mate. He knows what he wants and that's who he's out looking for. It does

no good to be all in his face if its not you that he adores. That's why its always best to sit back and see

what he does. If its not you, oh well. Next. Your man will one day come through the door. If you are

his interest, still follow his lead ,and, before long you should be planning a future together. A marriage

together. A life together. Remember. These are Gods men and He has all types. Take the time to know yourself and then you'll know when you've met your match. When you do and when its right you

both will know. He won't be married. He won't play games. He's looking for his wife just as you're

trying to find your husband. Sit back. Be patient. Not every man is right for you, so, when a good man

appears and he chooses you . . . make sure that he's the man that you choose too. Good luck to all of us

 in search, one day when we least expect our man will show up.

Chemistry With A Good Man

ENTERING THE ROOM, all male eyes are on me. Showered, clean and giving off a real pleasant scent from a splash of my favorite perfume. I'm poised, confident, groomed and look good from head to toe. Even in casual wear, I'm sharp, well put together and coordinated from top to bottom. This is just how I dress. Eyes glare from everywhere as I try not to notice. I take my seat and when I do decide to look up there are one pair of eyes in particular looking straight through me and at close view. Like he is reading the inside of my heart and soul. It is like he can see right through me. It's too late to move or try to hide and dive because the process is already in progress before I even looked up. I try to look away, play it off, shake it off, but, the chemistry is too strong to deny. Too strong to fight. It's just right there, it can't be ignored or over looked. Something totally strange. Something totally unfamiliar is in the air. You begin to wonder what are his thoughts when you realize you are having thoughts of your own. The chemistry is so strong, so powerful, so wow that you're both taken by surprise. I don't know what is going on here, but obviously he likes what he sees. I'm thinking, fine by me cause I'm feeling the same chemistry. There is a very strong force, a very strong emotion that is knocking us off our feet. We just sit and stare. I don't know how he feels but I hope he won't go anywhere. The feeling I'm feeling just feels good, it feels right. It feels like we're absolutely in heaven. I guess he must be feeling the same way because when he does walk away, he at no time at all comes right back. Each time he does, I'm so excited I could bust, but, I wonder what could this be. With every smile, with every raise of the eyebrow a deeper connection is being made. It's like we're extracting from one another our thoughts and feelings. Uncovering the hurt and pain. Sharing love and thoughtfulness. Fulfilling emptiness. Satisfying the loneliness without ever speaking a word. I don't know his name or a thing about him. Only what he makes me feel. As I continue to look into his eyes, I feel like a woman. A beautiful woman. Like a woman being loved. I feel elegant, intelligent, complete. Over time and with each passing day you become content, happy, peaceful, pleased. You notice there is nowhere else he would rather be than around you, and, you notice you miss him when he is not. You notice he doesn't have that same strong interest in other women. He is into you. Because you are into him as well, other men don't seem to have an appeal. The two of you are in this alone. You're in it together and outside forces aren't allowed. They can't phase us. They don't penetrate. I watch him as he grows stronger and stronger and as he gets deeper and deeper into our relationship and I see, his eyes are definitely on me. I continue to dress and recreate my awesomeness each and every day. Keeping him totally satisfied is my goal. It's a joy and something I love to do. As I look I see him putting in those same efforts every day for me. I hope and pray that this will never end. Now that the relationship has its foundation. Now that our undying attraction has developed into love.

Now that our emotions have been in sink all along, we both should be desirous of marriage to one another. In the beginning when I walked in the room, sat down and looked up, he was already smitten. One day soon you'll look up to a ring being placed on your finger. One day soon you will say I do to the man you have your chemistry with.

SECTION THREE

Single Men

I KNOW YOU read the chapter about us getting prepared and ready. How we're working on becoming better and to be more pleasing. More pleasant. The question that we all have though is, what are you going to do. As women are going through self development and becoming all we can be for our own self growth and satisfaction. To meet Gods approval most definitely. There is that one other reason that we do all that we do. As you already know . . . it's for you. As we mature. As we evolve from good, better, best, our man will need to be there when we reach the top. We are expecting you to be well groomed. Well mannered and full of chivalry. Just as we already know and you should too . . . the best is for the best. Just as we're in the gyms working our butts off for that oh so nice figure. In the hair salons the entire day for that perfect hair style, but, not complete until our nails and toes are just as beautiful. We're praying, meditating, reading self help books. Cooking, cleaning and purchasing our outfits . . . matched from head to toe mind you. Smelling good and looking totally awesome. All of it to benefit and satisfy ourselves of course but also with the hopes that one day you will come along and we will take your breath away.

Men. We do all that we do because it's what we should do. We're trying to grow as a person and into very beautiful women. Into a very mature, a very beautiful person. We all should be attempting to better ourselves with each and every day that we live. We should all be trying to be the best person we can be, etc. In the end though when we look around and everything is in its place, clean and shinning. Brilliant pictures on the wall of different events and accomplishments. Closets full of gorgeous outfits, one after the other. Homes purchased along with some of the best looking cars parked in the driveway. Money saved. All this and on and on. A woman still needs her man. All of its great, but, it all becomes marvelous when her man is seated at the table next to her. When we both buckle our seat belts before we pull out the driveway going wherever together. When we are both planning our futures filled with all the things we both want. When we're both thanking our Lord for what He's blessed us with. The end to every perfect day is to thank our Lord for allowing us the pleasure of finding one another. So. Men. God is blessing His women to become the best we can be for you. Be prepared and don't resist Him as He works His way into your heart. As he comes into your lives to make you ready and right for us too. As I mentioned before. Marriage is actually a command from God. Now. You can ignore Him as most of you do. Continue to use women for your little boyish and immature games. Continue to break our hearts and our wallets too. Keep sleeping around with your woman's mother, her sisters, her aunts and the other women down the same street. Continue to sleep with women around the corner and on your woman's job. Have babies with all of them. Lie to them all. Give them all aides. Continue to do all the madness you do. Only you know what that is. Only you because of course the ones involved in your bull are too dumb to figure it out. You're the only brilliant one in the equation. Well, that's what you think in your own little head. So. For years and years and years, you just play women like we're toys. Really we're not even as relevant as your precious toys are to you. Your little black books are shameful. The way you regard women is shameful, and, your conduct on God's green earth towards his women has been shameful. Even though it's no excuse, it's all by design just as how the women have fallen has been by design. It's all one great big scheme of the devil. The strategy the powers that be have exercised on us. We must give the wicked ones credit because they did their job one hundred percent. To the thousandth degree. Black man . . . just as you have been using, dogging and manipulating your own women . . . satan used you to do it. This is the condition that we've been put in by someone wiser than us. We must now realize it, be just as wise and straighten things out. Now that we know not only has the woman been used but you too, now that we realize we have all been played one against the other . . . we also now know that we have our work cut out. Women now realize some of the behaviors we have as women are damaging and you too must realize that everything satan says is alright to do is by far not alright. Not only is it not alright but its completely destructive. Destruction we will feel for generations to come, and generations after those if we as individuals don't have the love and courage it takes to put a stop to all our lose ways. Our futures. Our children's futures. Their children's futures depend on it. We need to all start now to do what we can to change things. We all have to start making better choices. Remember that just because we want something or someone does not necessarily mean that we need it. Wants and needs are entirely two different things. If what we want will bring us nothing but shame and disgrace in the morning or years later when we're sitting there trying to explain our foolishness to our children, why they shouldn't do as I did just do as I say . . . just don't do it in the first place. Process of elimination. Let our intelligence prevail . . . not our ignorance and or weakness for satan and his ways.

A Man's Role In A Childs Life

BECAUSE YOU CARRY the seed of life. You are where all life comes from. The creator gave you an awesome, powerful gift, but, that gift comes with an awesome, powerful responsibility. Not something at all to take lightly. You have to be really super careful on how you handle things. How you live your life. The relationships you involve yourself in. The children you make. We put them at such a disadvantage when the parents are no longer together. When they no longer speak due to differences and separation. When the father walks out period, never to be seen again. The children grow up with a certain loneliness. A certain desperation for their dad. A certain need that only the father can fulfill. The same would apply if the mothers not there. It takes two to make the children and it really does take two to raise them. Now I know we all make do with what we have just as I had to do in raising my children without their dad being in the home after our divorce. Even though he always helped out and remained a part of the children's life, the struggle would not have been as hard if we were both working inside the home as one solid force. If you slow your roll some. If you were to take the mating act a little more seriously. If you took a woman a little more seriously. If you had a little more love and respect for yourself, one less child would be born into an unbalanced home. Growing children need input, love, guidance and finances from the father as well as their mother. Women can't be men even when we think we can. We can't be men just as men can't be women. When children are being raised the role the man plays in the family unit is just as important as the role the woman plays. Men and women play different roles in the child's life but both roles are extremely important and both roles are extremely needed for the child's development. They are both equally needed. Both parents are needed to bring balance into a child's world. Each parent adds something different to the child's life. Each parent serves a different purpose and both influences are very vital for the child. Men help teach their daughter what real love is by the love he shows her. He teaches her what a real man is by the way he treats and respects her mother. A father keeps the hound dogs away so that his daughter can grow up to be the woman God wants her to be. Minus the traps, pitfalls and hell a girl goes through in her young life without the guidance and protection of her father. The father helps his daughter understand the opposite sex . . . good and bad. A father carefully, cleverly guides his daughter away from a harmful lifestyle with men into a successful, respectful life with men. In particularly her man when God blesses her to find him. Of course we know the man in a boy's life is crucial. When the male figure is absent in the home, the male in the home has no figure to follow. Just as when the woman is absent in the home and the girls have no image for themselves. If girls were to take on their fathers image-then this is not who they were born to be. If the men are not there for their boys and the boy takes on his mother's image. Later on down the road he's walking around on a national talk show in his moms dress and high heels telling you and everyone else listening that this is just the way he was born. Meanwhile our other son is out on the corner in a gang because these are the only males they have to look up to. The only men around to help address his growing manhood. We already know this type character he has been made into by the streets for the lack of a better one by his dad is going to make him have to work triple hard to qualify for a good woman, if it's even his desire to do so. He may turn out so thugged out that he has zero respect for the female and prefers to be our pimp when he gets out of prison. The mother as a result stays in the court room until sentencing because he's charged with selling drugs, stealing purses and cars. From there, the mom runs back and forth from jail cell to jail cell. Not to even mention, she's desperately fighting back the tears on an every minute basis because she just buried one of your siblings for the same above gang banging madness. All at the same time trying to raise the others so that they don't turn out like the above. In their same situations. All at the same time trying to hold down her job, because, whatever, whatever, everyone still has to eat. On and on and on because a woman's work is never done, but, where are you. We don't even really have to ask, because, of course, you're out making another baby. The only solution is for men to become serious again about women. Become serious again about their responsibility in life. Once that happens, this type book won't be necessary. Those of you who aren't very serious . . . grow up and quit playing because our life is at stake. For all the men who are already handling their business with their woman and family, thank you. Keep up the good work. Let your light shine.

The world is set up for men to use women in whatever way you please. If you decide to rape us, it's okay. If you want to use us for your baby mama and never commit to us, it's okay. Use and disrespect us on all or whatever level and its okay. When you sit around laughing at and about us while you tally all of it up in your little black books, it's okay. Well. In reality it is not okay when men are committing these evils on your mother, your sister, your aunt. Nor is it okay when you commit them on other females of your choice. This is why we're in the situation we're in as people. As a nation. The entire world is suffering behind ridiculous conduct. It is not okay. It's self destructive. Look around and watch our society breaking down all due to acts of evil. When you deliberately set out to misuse mistreat or to take advantage of a woman or anyone for that matter. Its evil. You may feel like they shouldn't be dumb enough. Naive enough. Weak enough. Vulnerable enough to let it happen. Maybe so, but, those are their problems and issues. Your problems and issues begin when you take advantage of the disadvantaged. The bread truck pulls up, the driver gets the bread he needed off the truck, leaves the door open to the truck while he runs in the store. You have access to all the bread you need for months to come. Do you take the bread. You're walking along and you notice that someone left the keys in the ignition to their car. There is absolutely no one else around and the car is even one of your favorites. Do you steal it. The point is . . . temptations. Easy set ups. The opportunity to do wrong is always present. The key though is for you to be stronger than the opportunity presenting itself. Another extremely important key is to guard against temptation when at all possible, meaning to be careful enough not to set your own self up in certain situations. I think they call it (staying out the way). Certain things in our own personal lives can be avoided. Certain situations you shouldn't even allow yourself to be in. Don't participate in the madness going on all around you. It is all based on principles, morals, values, self respect. I'm sure I'm not the first person you've heard this from. If so, hope you get my drift on this and conduct your lives on a higher level. Wrong is wrong in whatever way it comes, the goal is to try not to get caught up, doing wrong. Period. I know it's easier said than done, but, practice makes perfect. For the old, old players all the way to the pimp with the most women and the most money . . . God knows all about you. If things stay the same, He'll be speaking to you next. Yes. I'm referring to our Lord. He doesn't approve of His women being mistreated. Nothing more needs to be said on this subject other than . . . men get it together in regards to women or, it won't even help to watch your back.

We know that if the woman doesn't clean up her act there is a price to pay. Women are actually paying it as we speak. You are smart enough to know you have a price to pay for the mess you've made. Take a look around at your women and children. Take a look at our present condition. This is your price for your misconduct. How do you begin to correct the wrongs. Get your morals together number one. Get your lives together by cutting out the lies. The deceit. The games. The foolishness. Cut out all the bull you do and align your life with the creator. He is your Father. Our Father and we must do what the Master said do. He made you therefore you can't out think Him. You can't out do Him. You can't override Him. Overlook Him. Kick Him to the curb like you do women. Wait. Of course you can because this is what you've been doing your entire life. Even though you may not have meant it that way, or maybe you did. Whatever your case is, take it up with Him today. Now. Because you have ignored His word and you have ran over His woman just as if we're nothing. Now is when to go to Him and beg for his forgiveness. When you get finished, go back again. Again and again until your crazy ways change. Until you're living a life that's pleasing to Him. Not you. Him. If you are deliberately, recklessly hurting women and children as a result, Gods not pleased. Until you're in accord with His will, pray. Continue to pray. Continue to pray. You know sounds and thoughts travel on the air waves, so, the minute you think a thought, the minute you say what you're thinking, it goes out there to God and His people. His angels. Believe me, they are all on their job just like we're on ours when we go to work every day. First, second or third shift. Whenever you pray with sincerity, He and the angels go to work on our behalf. Even when your prayers don't manifest right away the gods are on their post. Be on yours by continuing to pray and sooner or later the results become obvious. Don't give up. While you're falling on your knees to come up out of this grip this savage acting enemy has on us . . . sisters will be falling on our knees too. When God decides to forgive us, then, we're ready to do as He said . . . meet and wed. Those same things that women are looking for and steering away from in men are the same things men should look for and steer away from in women. I'm sure most of you know, but for those who don't . . . there are wicked, evil women out here. Women that will lie to you. Deceive you. Use and manipulate you. Break your heart into pieces and then throw the pieces away as if nothing ever happened. Don't let pretty faces, batting eyelashes and sexy ways fool you. Look behind all that and get to know her, keeping in mind that opposites attract. Just as women should always be careful when someone is attracted to them, so should you be. Don't automatically fall in head over hill with all your feelings. All your money and everything you own. Take the time to know her. See if she is trustworthy. See if she is worth your time. Figure out if she is your true mate. Not just a mate, but, a true mate. Again. Just as we as women have to be careful with you so do you as men fooling with some of us. With that being said. Of course we all know that there are many, many very beautiful women out there. They are beautiful inside. They are beautiful outside. They are highly intelligent and they have the utmost love and respect for men in general and will therefore have the utmost love and respect for her man. Don't play games with her. Don't hurt her because she doesn't deserve that. Just sit back, be cool and leave her alone if feelings for her aren't mutual. Remember.

While you are out and about doing your dealings amongst women, remember to be careful. Remember. Gods watching. He is who we all answer to. Since you men, lead the whole situation . . . know where you're headed in life before approaching one of us. We're working on being ready when you do. May God bless us both men and women to make the right choice. When its right. When she is good for you. When you're the right fit for her, we then become a team. Two is stronger than one and together our love will shine as bright as the sun. If we were good on our own, when we join forces there is nothing that can't be done. We should at this point move to take the next step . . . marry her because you have found the best. We will know that we've been blessed when God takes us in His arms. When He spreads His love and charm throughout our home because He Himself approves of our commitment. With Him backing us, our union can't go wrong. He Himself will keep us strong all because we're doing His will. That in itself grants our success and a life filled with all His best.

Our Brother Our Man
We Appreciate You

EVEN THOUGH WE sometime may not see eye to eye. We appreciate you.

Even though we know you're trying, the sister is still behind doors crying but knowing it's all a matter of timing because our brother, our man is now standing. We appreciate you.

Even though our enemy bought you down, put you to sleep and would kill you before he allowed you to wake . . . your sister will push you up, rush you up, back you up and at the end of the day, your wife will love you up. We appreciate you.

Brothers. Listen up! Be strong. Be confident. Don't worry about a thing as you stand to take your place back as king. Stand tall and be proud that God chose you to help bring in His new world. That is an absolute honor. You should most definitely feel flattered. We appreciate you.

As you work hard and even harder to do His will, remember . . . sisters are your support system and with God's help you will surely win. You are our kings and our dear friends and we love you. We stand by you our brother our man.

Girls Grow Into Roses

WHEN WE'RE LITTLE we're real cute with pigtails and little girl forms. We know right away how to smile

and act and use our little girl charm. We grow up curious, smart and bright, very much adored. Before

we know we can cook and sew among all the other things we learned. We take a strong interest in

how we look, our hair, our nails, our wardrobe. We learn who we are what we like and want and

develop a very strong will to acquire our desires. We go to work on all type levels to achieve what we

set out to be. We work hard to get things just right to ensure that we remain happy. We're very careful

to make sure at all times that God is pleased. We carry ourselves with love and respect and become the

most beautiful rose we can be. We become the most beautiful rose you can find, and, we do it for both

you and me.

SECTION FOUR

Is A Good Woman Hard To Find

WE HANDLE OUR business as women. We're good at it, truly cold with it. Running the house. Raising the children to the best of our abilities. Working in and outside the home. Paying the bills. Buying the meals. Dressing for success and to impress making sure our loneliness is at all times suppressed. We come big, bad, strong ready to take on and tackle the world. By this worlds design we have been made to step up. If the man is not present and even a lot of times when he is, the woman has no choice but to step up. If the man is in the home but has lost his job. Or in the home but he is not at the particular time able to handle the whole load for whatever the reason, the woman is made to step up. This has been going on for decades now. For decades, with each step we make it helps the family on one hand, everyone has to eat, but, on the other hand it is quietly, subtly tearing the family apart. Along the way, we have become hard, bold, aggressive. We don't need anyone. We don't need any help and in some women's case, especially from a man. Why. A lot of us have become pretty little men. Some of us are gay and that is what they choose, but, some of us don't even realize that they are very manly. A lot of subtle changes are going on. By design, the household, the family is breaking down, breaking up. We're strong, independent and make a lot of money. This along with the wrong mentality is deadly to the family structure. In a lot of homes, in a lot of ways, the man is getting pushed further and further out of the picture even if he is sitting right there. We know everything coupled with false pride and arrogance . . . there is nothing a man can do that I can't do better. Move, I'll do it. Just shut up, I can do it better. The level of disrespect, inconsideration and flat out rudeness are out the wazoo. Even though it's all by design and we as women were forced to step up in order to hold the family down . . . there is a price that we are all now paying. I'll run a few of them by you.

1. Hell, she wants to be a man. I'll let her do just that. Now he sends you off to work each morning while he talks on the phone all day, in the chat room, face book or whatever else he does while you're out making a living. Something is clearly wrong with that picture. God made men to provide for the women and children, not the other way around.

2. She doesn't have one ounce of respect for me, but, I know who does, and, your man don't come home cause he is with her.

3. She can do it all on her own, so, do it. He won't help around the house at all, period. He is laying around flicking channels and well rested while you're over worked, stressed out and broke down.

4. He is there but wishes he wasn't. He is dreaming of someone that is not like you.

5. Everyone is unhappy, unfulfilled and the divorce rate is sky high. Wait. It gets even uglier because we forgot the children are watching what we say and do, so, all of this has a residual effect for more decades to come. Except there is one more important difference . . . each generation gets worse so says the bible. So what is going on now will look like child's play to their children. This is the point. There is a serious problem that lies with us as women, and, as women, we must begin to address it. We must work and do our best at trying to solve it. Even if we were made to step up, we are still women and our men are still our men. If we show a little more respect towards ourselves and our men, that in its self will help to change things towards the way they should be. Back down a little, soften up a little, lady up a little. Remember. We're searching for love. Remember.

Good men are not trying to be with another man, they are the man already. Men are looking for women. A good man is searching for a good woman. There should be a distinct difference between the two of us. In other words, women should act like women, not men. If we're too manly, this is the area we need to go to work in like immediately. Become more womanly, it is who God made us to be and we want to become the best at who we are. Of course, the same applies to the men. There should be a distinct difference between the two of us. Men should act like men the role God gave you. If you are not manning up, this is the area you need to go to work in immediately. Don't fool around wasting time-enough damage has already been done and we're actually sabotaging our own happiness. We're holding our own self back in the romance department. Once we get things together and straightened out . . . love and your soul mate will be standing in your face. Keep in mind . . . we are some ones soul mate, we want to be on point whenever we do meet. Once our feminine side steps up, it will bring out his manhood and everything else will fall into place. We have to get back to who we really are, the kings and queens on earth. Both men and women need to go to work on self and stop letting our happiness pass us by. If we can survive the (jail cell four hundred year sentence) better known as slavery, we can certainly do this and anything else we put our minds to. Something that will help us. Something just for us. We have helped everyone else since we've been here. Now it's our turn to help ourselves. Once we put our energy into it, our men will be looking at nothing but excellence. Just like our ancestors . . . because of their own self respect and because they knew how to treat their men, their men responded accordingly. Turning all this madness back around is in our very own hands as women. Because remember, our men respond to us. The reward will be never ending. For the women who already have it together thank you for the example you set because some of us need all the help we can get. If you ask me, we're in a very exciting position. A position that will turn our history back around to where and how it should be. Let's do it for ourselves. Let's do it for our men. Let's do it for our children. Let's do it because God says so. So, let's do it to save our lives. If men think we're desirable now, wait until we're done. Just wait. Wait to see the women we become.

Becoming Even More Desirable

1. If you're married but separated, you're still married. Divorce your spouse before you take one more step so that you don't end up in an adulterous relationship. Not only is adultery forbidden by God, but, if you're cheating on your spouse which is exactly what it is because you are not divorced. If you're cheating on your spouse, why would the person you're cheating with trust that you wouldn't do them the same way. Why would you trust that the person you're cheating with won't turn around some day at some point and then cheat on you. Without trust there is nothing which means you are already starting off on the wrong foot sabotaging what could have been. Messing the relationship up from the very start. Don't involve an innocent person that has nothing to do with your situation and your unfinished business. If you're no longer in love with your spouse. If things in your marriage are not working to your satisfaction and you've tried everything you could. If year after year you continue to be unhappy for reasons that are grounds for divorce, then, divorce is what you should do before starting up another situation with someone else. First things first. One thing at a time. Also take some time to regroup before moving so quickly into another disaster. Take some time to figure out what went wrong in the relationship on your part so as not to repeat the same mistakes in your new marriage. The goal in marrying someone is that that person is to be your mate for life. If you have had one failed marriage, you certainly want to take some time with yourself to properly prepare

in order to have a successful second marriage. Marriage is not a game to see how many I marry in my lifetime. Single people. If you're in a relationship that's not working for you, end it before you start up another one. Keep your relationships separate, one relationship at a time, not, how many can I juggle at a time. We're looking for real love not, oh, my life is a joke. It makes it that much harder to commit to one when there are several to choose from-everyone has something good about them. Everyone has something different and interesting about them and when you are talking with more than one person at a time, a decision is harder to make. Especially if feelings develop for each it's hard to let go of either or any of them. As a result, you can't make a decision so you end up stuck with all of them, never able to have that one serious, precious relationship you long for in your heart.

2. Your hearts been broken and its left you bitter. Mend your heart before you get involved with the next person. Get rid of all that attitude and negativity before you involve yourself with someone new. They had absolutely nothing at all to do with your previous situation and it's not fair to take your anger out on them. Besides. This could be the right one and you don't want to push them away with your messed up attitude toward them. An innocent person who has done nothing-absolutely nothing in the world to you.

3. If you doubt love will ever come your way, you're helping to sabotage your own chances of finding your true love. We get back what we put out into the atmosphere, into the universe. So, we think positive and know that love is on its way to finding you. The fact that love finds someone each and every day and has every since God made men and women shows us that we have a one hundred percent chance. In fact men and women finding one another is Gods whole point of creating us in the first place. This is all the proof we need. Love will find us. How, when, where becomes the question, but, not if. Everything in life is based

on timing. If true love has not knocked yet maybe we need to truly get prepared because, it is on its way. Especially if love is what you're praying for. If its love we're seeking, we need to be ready for it when it gets here.

4. The sooner we get rid of all the negatives of the past, the better off we will be. Get rid of the anger, the hurt, the pain so that it doesn't become a part of your personality. We have to chalk the past up as life's experiences. Lessons learned. Training ground. The real bottom line . . . they are all the things that shaped us into who we are. They have made us into the strong beautiful people that we have become. We have to learn to take it all in stride and look at life and our experiences from a positive point of view. It is Gods way of making us into who we need to be and believe me He knows what He's doing. Personal experiences and everyone experiences something different because it's our own individual and personal lesson . . . making an awesome individual when it is all said and done. Of course if we don't get the positive from it, we let it break us and we become ugly acting, closed off, bitter. All the above and some. However awful the experience was or is when its understood and when the dust clears something good will come from it. That's if we're positive enough to receive it. Not having a pleasant attitude could be a turn off and could prevent or hinder someone from becoming interested. You don't want to appear unapproachable if you are a woman because men won't approach you. If you're angry and unapproachable as a man, women won't want you. Stuck up and snobbish people. If you're a stuck up person and that's really just you. A trait that's been passed down in your DNA, your mate can handle that. Snobbish is rudeness, a character flaw and a turn off to most people in general. Come down a little and work at becoming just a little more humble. A little less ugly acting. A little less uppity. No one owes you anything and a lot of people won't pay the price of being with you. We're trying to find a mate. Right. Not send them running and never return again.

5. Not too manly ladies. He is the man. We're the women. Control some of the aggressiveness. He is not looking for a woman that's more manly than himself. Even if we're not in need of a man we all still want to be the best people we can be, the best woman we can be. Right. This helps us to be more attractive. Beauty is not based on looks alone. When we carry ourselves in a pleasant, kind, respectful way you automatically become more attractive. People normally like warmth, not too cold. Not too hard but not too easy. By easy I mean point blank, too quick to go to bed with them. You don't want to be used for bootie calls. Don't be quick to give him your money, car keys and the house. You're trying to become a wife not his fool. Men the same goes for you too. Don't get played, don't get used.

6. We must become skilled. Catching a good mate takes a certain skill. Some people are born with the skill and it comes naturally and others have to learn the skill. It all boils down to how you handle and carry yourself. Realize that as an individual person, you're special, unique and you would be a pleasure for anyone to meet. Not arrogant and boastful, just confident in yourself. Confident in who you are and you don't go out of your way to be noticed. Your overall appearance at first glance, your persona when you enter the room is the attraction. Now, let's keep in mind that everyone won't be attracted to you regardless nor do you want everyone to be attracted to you. You only want to attract one person in particular. The right one for you. You go through the changes of finding just the right outfit when you're on your way to wherever. Make sure we're showered, shaved, smell good. Our persona takes over and does the rest. It's what makes someone accept you, attracted to you, desire you. If everyone in the room is dressed just as nice or better. They look just as nice as you or better. They smell just as nice as you or better, but, you get chose. How did that happen . . . it's your persona. They like what they see. They like what they feel from you. Everyone has their own individual persona and that's why you're attracted to some people and some people you're not

attracted to. This all happens before you meet, before you speak. It's all in how you carry yourself. How confident are you, how much self respect do you have. How much self esteem do you have. How much class do you have and how well can you keep your composure. We don't make fools out of ourselves for someone or anyone. A person is either attracted to you or their not. This being said, as women we don't need to go out of our way to get a person's attention, a person's approval by flirting, chasing, harassing. This type behavior is beneath us. This type behavior is also why we get taken advantage of. We're much, much too good for all that. Our vibe either catches him-whoever or it doesn't. If not, they're not our man. Your man will be attracted to you. If a man is not attracted to you, he is not the man for you, and, it's okay because feelings need to be mutual. Your mans on the way. You don't want to be caught up in a miss matched relationship. You want to be the match for your mate and your mate needs to be a match for you. You never settle for someone who doesn't really want you for real. We are queens and that's how we need to be treated. So don't panic. Don't worry. Don't stress. All you really need to do is be you. Your man will take it from there. If a man is attracted to you, the only thing left to do at that point is to see if you feel the same attraction for him. As for men, if it feels right, pursue her and see where it leads. The same advise goes for men also though. Don't stay and keep tolerating a disrespectful woman. If she can't treat you like her king and the way a king should be treated, let her go. There are plenty women out here who would love to have you. Everyone is looking for what they are looking for. Pretty or not. Light, dark or in between. Large, small. Well dressed or not that into clothes. Beauty is in the eye of the beholder. It's based on an individuals preference and desire, number one. Number two . . . along with your appearance working for you on one hand, your personas working for you on the other hand. This leaves all of us with the same chance and the same opportunity to find a mate. The only thing in our way is the correct timing. When will we meet, only the love gods know the answer to that. Love is in the air though. Just breath it in. My soul mate is out there just waiting to be found so I will ask the love gods to send you to me. In the meantime, I will just focus on being the best person I can be. The more developed, mature, accomplished and successful we are is the level your mate will be on, if not more so. Focus on being as attractive as we can because you never know when your mate will show up. Ladies, when he does show up . . . asking your name, phone number, address and sleeping with you is not the first thing he does. The absolute first thing he does is notice you. He sees you first. Your persona is in effect and he is watching. A lot of times they see us and watch us way before we realize they are watching. Way before they approach us. So, we want to always carry and present ourselves the way we want him to ultimately treat us. We carry ourselves with respect. We carry ourselves with high regard. This is also the way we dress. Rather we know he's watching or not, we've already sent him a clear message, and, believe me, he received it. When he steps to you it will be in a respectful manner with the correct intent. If by chance signals get crossed and mixed up somehow on his end and he doesn't approach you respectfully, chances are he is mixed up and crossed up himself and please let him go back where he came from. If he didn't use enough thoughtfulness to even try and introduce himself to you, how much thoughtfulness will be used in the relationship. Be patient and wait on the right one. Everyone that approaches you may not be for you. They may like what they see and desire you, but, if the feelings not mutual let him go and hold out for the right man. He is coming, hold on. We don't base our decision on desperation for a man, our decision is based on the man's character. Is his character as suave as mine. Of course, men, the same applies to you. Check out her character.

6. Ladies. While we wait we will get better and better prepared. Don't walk around appearing desperate, anxious

and searching even though we are. Hold your pretty head up. Carry yourself with confidence. Carry yourself with grace. Ladies, if at some point you actually see someone you're attracted to, remember, let him make the first move. Remember. This shows if he is attracted to you, not just you feeling him, because, remember, it takes two.

Cherish Your Marriage
Cherish Your Love

———————

ONCE YOU'RE BLESSED to find your mate, that's exactly what it is, a blessing. Don't take your mate and your marriage for granted. You won't want to blow it, lose it and then regret it. God commands marriage, so once the decision to be together is made, marriage should come next. There is no negotiation here. It's a command and both of you should see to it. Of course you want your wedding to be beautiful, memorable and make sure it is. Afterwards though is when your lives begin. From that point on your works already cut out. The beginning of a balancing act. Until now there has been just you to deal with, just you to consider. Now there is two, and, a lot of times your spouse comes before you. Ladies. There will be times when you don't feel like doing your hair or dressing up, but, you do. Times when you don't want to be awakened in the middle of the night for different or whatever reasons, but, you get woke up. It seems you cook every meal that's ever been invented in one weeks time. You wash until the washer and dryer both break down. If the wife works outside the home, life would be easier if both the husband and the wife would share in the cooking and household chores. After all marriage is a partnership. If she doesn't work outside the home but she is raising your children, still help around the house, it is your house as well as hers. Raising a family is a twenty four hour a day job . . . you never really get a break. When she takes your shirts and suits back and forth to the cleaners so that their clean for you to wear to work. When she cooks your breakfast and packs your lunch so that you are nourished enough to work. When she rubs your aching back and feet from working too much. When you come home all stressed out and tense from work and she helps you relax in that one way . . . she is helping you. Every bit of it and some is what a good wife does and that's all very good. Marriage is a partnership though and if either one of you finds ways to help the other in the struggles they may be going through, well, it just makes a better marriage. Sacrifice after sacrifice will be made throughout your marriage. The thing is though, whatever it is you do for your spouse should always be pleasing to you. It is all an expression of love to your spouse because of course you do love them. As long as your mate is trying just as hard to please you, your marriage will blossom into a very beautiful, very long lasting union. You gave up the worldliness and totally hanging with the crowd the day you married your spouse, if not before. You venture out from time to time to enjoy and have some fun, but, when you're done you're back at home making it a better and happier place for both of you to be. The battlefield is outside the house and should never be brought inside the home. Your home environment should at all times be peaceful, clean, pleasant. A place you enjoy being, a place you love to come home to. This is the inside and the beginning stages of your very own private heaven. Your sanctuary. Once we step into heaven, we have to work to stay there. We have to work to maintain that status, because, angels do fall too . . . that is, if you are one. If not, the average person can fall down as we all know. Heaven is only for the worthy. Your marriage can be heavenly if you make it that way, or, it can go the other way and you both will be sitting directly in the middle of hell not being able to stand the sight of one another. Not only do you have to pray a lot to keep what God has blessed you with, you also have to put a lot of thought into how to keep it. Peace is a natural state, but, in an evil and turmoiled world . . . hard to find and even harder to maintain. Both spouses should work hard at keeping the devil out of your sanctuary. Work hard at keeping a happy home. Talk, communicate to find out what is working in the home and the relationship and what is not, and again, if we must sacrifice for the success of the union, sacrifice is what we do. Don't be quick to give up on one another, don't be quick to throw in the towel and run for a divorce. Thrive on the love that brought you together in the first place. Tell each other how much you love and appreciate one another. Show each other . . . love remember is an action word. Prove your love. Use your kindness. Your patience. Your understanding. Your thoughtfulness. Your empathy. In the meantime . . . you two are merging, blending, harmonizing way down in your souls. You're becoming one in your thinking. You're becoming one in your behavior toward one another, you're becoming one in your heart. You're becoming solid, strong, sturdy. You've become accustomed to one another. You're working through issues together, through your problems together, through your lives together. You hang in there with one another because it's a fight worth fighting. Its time well spent and the prize in the end is, you still have your dear friend. Don't fall prey to envious and jealous people who want what you have. When God sees fit, they will find true love too. It is not our call at all, it's out of our hands. Don't let them destroy what you've worked hard to get, build and working even harder to keep. Every ones turn will come when and if it is His will. In the meantime it is your turn to shine and do your thing as a couple, bringing hope to all on lookers and ultimately pleasing God. The pay off is for the two of you to be happy. Life is good when you have someone to share it with. When someone is working with you. When someone is right by your side. When your mate has your back every step of the way. Work on keeping your marriage tight, work at keeping it right and satisfying for the two of you. Whenever you may need to seek help or guidance make sure it is from those who care about love, not someone who really doesn't and is quick to tell you to give up. You've come too far to just turn around. Yes, you will struggle and go through hard times, but, that's the nature of marriage. Each struggle you're in and win. Each time you come through it together. Each time you push past the hardship, the marriage gets stronger and stronger. Emotionally you move to another level. As time and struggles persist, you are growing stronger as a couple, more confident as a couple, more harmonized as a couple. You're learning the do's and don'ts. What works and what won't. You're learning to give, to compromise, to be thoughtful, to be grateful, to be thankful. You bring out things in each other no one else can. This is your soul mate who gets down to the root of your core and helps you realize things about yourself you never knew. Things you chose to ignore are now starring you in the face. You're in the middle of total intimacy mentally, physically, spiritually. Do we like what we see . . . the majority yes which is why we fell in love to begin with, but, some things must go. Now what things. You two must decide between you what's what. Just be sure to hold onto whatever is good, right, positive and allows the union to grow. Sleep too much. Talk too much. Don't clean enough. Don't clean right. Not enough sex. I'm exhausted from too much sex. Whatever's needed to help the union grow and move to the next level. Marriage is hard work but it should be fun working to make things just right. Making your home a place you both love to be and can never wait to get back to. Making yourself just right so that there is nowhere else your spouse would rather be than right there with you. Build your marriage so good, so right, so tight that either of you stray away. Either of you are interested in committing adultery. When you cherish your love you both become real examples of what marriage and true love really is. Something we all need to see more of.

Once you have love, relationships, and marriage pretty well figured out, always be willing to help a struggling couple see their way through. Be willing to talk to teenagers and young adults about the importance of taking the time to find your soul mate and not just any and everyone who approaches you. Not just every good looking person that passes by. Explain the importance of commitment. The importance of marriage. These are the tools for strong, safe and respectful families, neighborhoods, communities, societies. Love is the key. If you are blessed with it, by all means let it shine. By all means . . . cherish your love . . . its God gift to you.

What God Has Joined Together

WHEN TWO PEOPLE are in love nothing else really matters. The sun shines brighter. The flowers more beautiful and life takes on a new meaning. One look into your eyes and all problems disappear. An instant calming affect that lets me know you are dear. Something in my soul says I'm yours and you're mine. The touch of your hand your smile and love from deep within activates the joy we share, you are my friend. I'm yours and you belong to me. The sound of your voice and your kind and caring ways create our very own paradise and only you and I can come in. Inside those walls are love, peace, tranquility. A love that's so strong it overcomes all obstacles and withstands the test of time. The kind of love that lets you know we are a match made from heaven. Love that says I'm yours and you're mine. Love that commands a commitment that comes from the fact that we both care. The kind of love that God brings together in holy matrimony. May God bless your union and may you have many, many years of happiness.

A MARITAL PLEDGE

WE SHOWER GOD with our love, our sacrifice, our hard work, our best. And when He is pleased with us, He smiles and takes care of all our needs. He with absolutely no doubt covers the rest and will bless us with many more years of marital bliss.

CLOSING THOUGHTS

NOW THAT MY thoughts on finding true love are coming to an end, I pray we are better satisfied. More equipped, a little more knowledgeable on how to handle the opposite sex. It all starts with self respect. Having a strong love for yourself and believe in doing unto others as you would want done. It's not about going after everyone we see or everyone that's attractive. It's really about sitting back. Practicing our patience until the love gods send our mate. Everyone in the city you live in is not your mate. Since there is only one, it can't be everyone. It's not anyone we meet and decide to greet and sleep with. Mating is not a little game that we play after work at happy hour. Or on the weekends as something to do just to kill boredom. Or to just add more names in your book as if this makes you a man or a woman. Real men. Real women are serious about who they give their attention to. They are serious about who they invite into their lives. Mature adults don't tolerate people running in and out of their heart and minds like you're running and operating a revolving door service. Really look in the mirror and start to love yourself. Accept yourself for who you are. Stop trying to be someone you're not born to be. Love yourself. If God made you, and, He did. No man. No race. No color makes hearts, tissues, muscles, eyes, ears. Imitations. Clones. Replicas. This is what man can do. The original you. The original me is Gods art. Who. What can top that. No one can. Anyone who tries only imitates. God is the creator. God is the originator. You can't top that. He can't be topped. If He took His time, love and creativity to make us . . . should we be ungrateful for the art He created. Should we be ungrateful and disrespectful to our self, to the person He made. That is rude and disrespectful to the creator

Himself. You make a vase as a gift to someone. You paint it just the right color and put a real special pretty, real pretty design on it. You even as a last touch engrave the person's name you're giving it to on the inside. You are so proud of it you don't know what to do. You spent your time on it. You put real thought into pleasing this person with every motion it took to create your special vase. You can't wait for your loved one to have it because it's so great. You're bubbling over with excitement as you present this precious work. You hand your work that you worked so hard on to the person you made it for with pride and admiration. Much to your shock and surprise because it's so uniquely made and beautifully designed . . . they hate it. They immediately go to work to destroy it. They change its color. Destroy the special very pretty design. In time the vase has absolutely no meaning to them what so ever. The last time you saw the vase you made, it was broken laying over in the corner on the floor. It's disregarded, unloved on every level. Imagine how you would feel if you made the vase. Your blood, sweat, and tears. Even deeper than that . . . your heart went into the vase. This is how God feels about each and every last one of us who have no love and respect, no regard for your own self. You are the vase that He made just for you to have throughout your days. He gave it to you when He put breathe into you and gave you your life. You hate yourself, His art and you are destroying His work through your everyday actions. Just as you would be hurt. Mad. Upset. Believe me. So is He. We need to watch the things we do. It's not wise to take yourself for granted. Sleeping around. Playing around. Taking yourself and each other for jokes. Using each other for pleasure and everything is a game . . . well first of all that is why we're in the boat we're in. Life is not any of this. It was never intended to be and it will come to an end. We understand that God created us. For this reason alone, we better smart up. If He created us and He's the creator number one and The Lord Of All The Worlds number two. What would that make us. His children. Right. Would a man master over everything be pleased with our low life, gutter conduct. The answer is . . . definitely not. Absolutely not. If our father is master of all things in the universe. Don't you think He deserves our respect. Don't you think He should have our respect. Until we give Him our respect, we will remain in the same boat. Disgracing ourselves fooling around. Once we begin to acknowledge and respect Him is the moment we begin to acknowledge and respect ourselves. Once we begin to love and honor Him is the moment we begin to love and honor ourselves. See the pattern. Put God first. Not this ridiculous foolishness we've all been involved in. Put God first. Ask Him to pull you up and keep you focused. Ask Him to pull you up. Ask Him to forgive your wayward, worldly ways. Ask Him for the strength to do better.

People. Our society has fallen apart and only God can help us rebuild it. Go to Him and change your heart. Once this part is done, we then all become available for one another. On the right level though. In a respectful way. In a loving, caring way. The ways that won't allow us to use and dog one another. Take each other for granted while we throw our hearts and bodies around and back and forth to one another. While we have all these children who have watched us. Studied us and as soon as they can, become us. Let's let those days be done. Let's let our father guide us to better ones. Let's let our father guide us to happier days. Let's be guided to a new type life where there is pure love in the air. Pure love in our natures. Pure love in our hearts. In our minds. Let God guide us to our true love. Once everything is in its right order, when things are coming from the proper perspective . . . good things happen. When God is first in your heart and life. When you love, respect and appreciate who you are because you are a gift from Him, the Lord and master of everything in creation . . . He can't be topped first of all and secondly, neither can you. When your mate walks up and walks by, they too will recognize. They will turn around, they will say, you are my mate. They'll know it. You will know it. You fit together like a hand and glove. Nothing can stop true love. Nothing can rock the two of you even when the angry ones try. Why. Because God made you for one another back when He first made you, and, because it was God who gave you permission to meet. This is why you both showed up to the particular occasion. The particular event where the two of you first met. It's all His doing. It's all His will. The love gods step in and help your love to ascend. The more you learn each other, the more you know it's true. When your heart swells to capacity with love for your mate. When your mind and soul aches for the mate that God made just for you, there are just two more things to do. First. Thank God for making this beautiful, magnificent piece of art that has such a love and devotion to me. Secondly. You must both follow His command. Get to the altar and be wed.

Our Children . . .
From the Youngest to the
Oldest and All Ages in Between

As WE ALL know, children are the end result of mating. Our children are the product of our love. Our little blessings. Our blessings that have been born into a world of misfortune on one hand. Children born with a purpose and a mission on the other hand. Our love for them molds and cultivates the person they have within. Our knowledge, experience and understanding is what helps build their attitude, character and thinking. The more in tune. The more in step we are as parents to what is what in life, the more helpful we are at giving our child a better start in life. We let them know from the start that we are Gods creation. We are Gods family. We explain with love and clarity that we're all here to do our part. The world we're born in is an absolute mess. A mess that they had nothing at all to do with. So no guilt trips on their part. We continue to explain that because God created us, gave life to us, we all have a duty to perform. Our work is not of fun and games. It's a little more serious than that. Although we do have our good times and our fun moments along the way and that will always be. To enjoy life is part of what life is all about and there is no doubt in that. There is the other side to life though that's not much talked about. It's not said that there is work we're born to and placed on earth to do. Now there are problems, situations and turmoil everywhere. The things I said earlier that you had nothing to do with, and it's all too much for any one person to handle. God can certainly do it all Himself, but, He wants us to become involved.

He wants us to prove our sincerity to Him so that He may decide. He wants to decide who He will invite in to live in His humble abode. The harder we work, the happier God gets and wow . . . we want to reach the goal. So what we first figure out is, what am I about. Whatever you do. Whatever you love is probably it. That's probably your niche. It's what God put in you. It's what He gave you to work on. It's what He gave you to work with. To build on until you perfect it. It is your one sure cure to help undo this mess. Of course discovering ourselves all takes time. None of it happens overnight. Real good people take time to perfect. So. We're learning, growing, expanding bit by bit. We're growing each day more and more into who we are. We learn a little through this and a little through that what life is really all about. Not so much fooling around with absolutely no aim. I see once I begin to look a little deeper that some things are already mapped out. As I continue to grow, learn and study I see that it's all quite clear. It's clear. A fact and no doubt that someone has succeeded in upsetting Gods planet. Someone has truly disturbed the world we live in. It's clear. A fact and no doubt that God is thoroughly upset with this mess. I see that there is obviously a battle going on between God and whoever the force is that made this mess. Of course I stand behind my Father and won't divorce. Once I figure out what part I play. Where I fit in this will be when my work begins. I have to remember. When He made us He put in us our own special gift. Our own individual talent. That's what we use to help straighten out this mess. We learn in school that scientist invent cures. Because God is the ultimate scientist, we are all Gods little baby scientist born to help invent everlasting cures. Cures on Gods behalf. In Gods favor. Now that we're aware of who we are, let's begin to act in accord. Now that we know our purpose in life, get aboard. Map out your plan and soar. Be all you can be and make the most and best of your life. Your entire family throughout the world backs you. As long as it's good. As long as it's right. You may use anything in the world to come up with your special potions. Your very own solutions. Yes. It's okay. You have permission because God owns everything, everything in the world. No, we don't take. We must always use our manners and we never forget to treat others the way we want to be treated. With that being understood . . .

God wants a change to be bought about. Everything. Everyone in Gods universe serves Gods purpose. Therefore, we won't be stopped. With all God's love and good luck. We're all the product of God's love. We return our love to Him by becoming the person God expects us to become. Bright, honest, strong and a delight. People born to handle our business with no excuse. We have our fun along the way but without losing focus. Never underestimate who you are and what you will accomplish. When it's all said and done. As time goes on and when it's our children's time to mate, world watch out . . . cause here comes all you can take.